CANADIAN CONTEMPORARY REPERTOIRE SERIES

FUN SELECTIONS OF JAZZ - POP - LATIN - FOLK

LEVEL ONE

CONSERVATORY CANADA™

For more information about Conservatory Canada
and its programs visit our website at:
www.conservatorycanada.ca

Office of the Registrar
Conservatory Canada
45 King Street, Suite 61
London, Ontario, Canada
N6A 1B8

ISBN 978-1-49500-536-7

Novus Via Music Group Inc.
189 Douglas Street, Stratford, Ontario, Canada N5A 5P8
(519) 273-7520 www.NVmusicgroup.com

Preface

Contemporary Canadian Repertoire is an exciting series of piano works by Canadian composers. Level One offers grade one students thirty -two appealing pieces at varied levels within the grade requirement. Students will develop technical and musical skills with user friendly repertoire from an entrance level to preparatory grade two works.

Repertoire selections have been based on grade appropriate keys, time signatures, accompaniments figures, degree of difficulty and length. Jazz styles include preparatory rags like *Paddling the Assiniboia* and *Tiny Tiger Rag*, which lead comfortably to *Icicle Rag* and *Rainy Day Rag* complete with stride bass, syncopated melodies and octave displacement. Boogies include works like *Jungle Band Boogie* and *Bass Boogie*. *Blues in My Soul* and *Got the Blues* provide varied accompaniments and blues scale playing. Students will be delighted by the swing rhythm of works like *Cowboy's Song*, *Ace of Spades* and *Sunflower and Sage Brush*. The lovely jazz ballad, *Hush Now*, jazz prelude *Otonabee River Song* and jazz waltzes, *Aeolian Jazz Waltz* and *Frozen Full Moon on a Sunday Afternoon* are just some of the jazz titles offered in this collection.

The ever popular work *Music Box Dancer* has also been included in this collection. Students will be rockin' to titles like, *Dinosaur Disco* and *Rock It!*, while Latin dance rhythms are included in works like, *Cheetha Cha Cha* and *Olè*. Arrangements of folk songs, *Citadel Hill* and *Brave Wolfe*, provide a strong sense of Canada's musical heritage, while the jazzed up version of *Twinkle Twinkle Little Star* and *Jazzin' Jupiter* is just plain fun.

Conservatory Canada wants to keep music students studying longer! We understand the benefits gained through the study of music and we believe that students will remain engaged and excited about their studies if that music is current and familiar.

This is why we developed the Contemporary Idioms curriculum. Students can now be assessed and accredited through a program that involves contemporary styles of music such as Swing, Blues, Latin and Rock.

Conservatory Canada supports Canadian composers. This book contains pieces that are either original compositions or arrangements by Canadian musicians. All the selections in this book are eligible for a Conservatory Canada Contemporary Idioms examination. The pieces have been chosen with attention to proper pedagogy, skill development and student appeal. We hope you enjoy them!

TABLE OF CONTENTS

Blues/Ballad

Rain .... Fishel Pustilnik 5
Daddy's Blues .... Fishel Pustilnik 7
Kind Wishes .... Fishel Pustilnik 13
Saga .... Fishel Pustilnik 19

Rock

Rock It! .... John Sandy 4
The Getaway .... Tyler Seidenberg 6
Ramble .... Fishel Pustilnik 8
Dinosaur Disco .... Janet Gieck 25
Snow Angel .... Janet Gieck 34

Swing

Frozen Full Moon .... Joyce Pinckney 9
Got the Blues .... Andrew Harbridge 10
On My Way .... Tyler Seidenberg 12
Bass Boogie .... Robert Benedict 14
Blues In My Soul .... Fishel Pustilnik 15
Cowboy's Song .... Andrew Harbridge 16
Aeolian Jazz Waltz .... Andrew Harbridge 22
Hush Now .... Joyce Pinckney 28
Ace of Spades .... Tyler Seidenberg 29

Other Genres

Rainy Day Rag .... Debra Wanless 11
Icicle Rag .... Joyce Pinckney 18
Otonabee River Song ...... Andrew Harbridge 20
Sunflowers and Sage Brush ... Joyce Pinckney 24
Brave Wolfe .... Fowke/Johnston (arr) 26
Olé .... Rémi Bouchard 30
Cheetah Cha Cha .... John Sandy 32
Citadel Hill .... Fowke/Johnston (arr) 33
Snow Angel .... Janet Gieck 34

Glossary of Jazz Idioms 35

Glossary of Terms 36

Rock It!

John Sandy

Not too fast

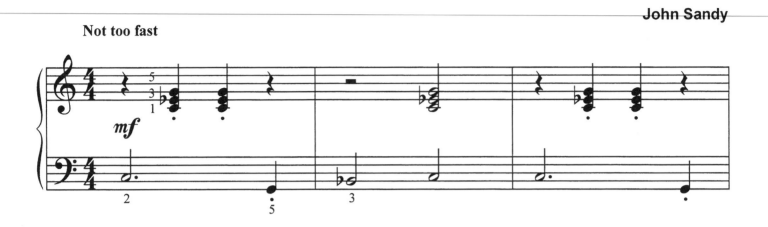

Rain

Fishel Pustilnik

Slowly, with expression

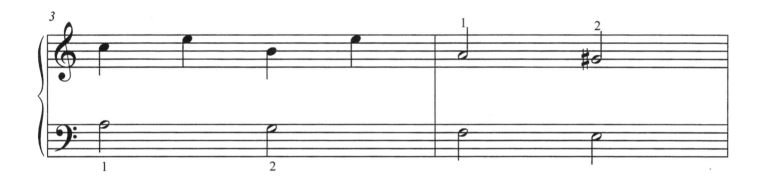

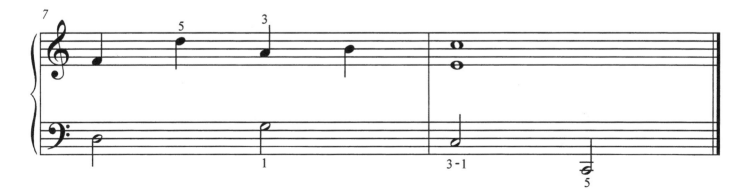

The Getaway

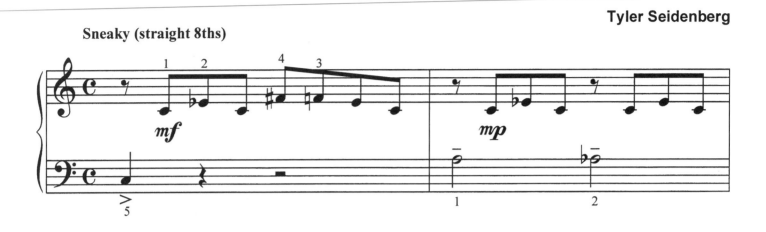

Tyler Seidenberg

Sneaky (straight 8ths)

Daddy's Blues

Fishel Pustilnik

Moderately, with a blues feel

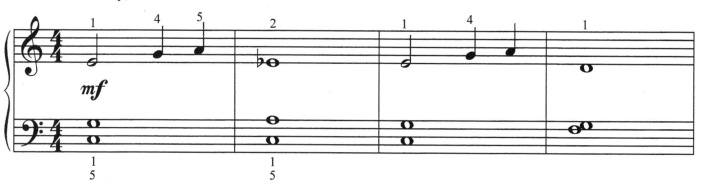

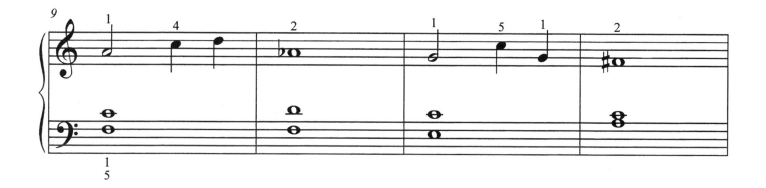

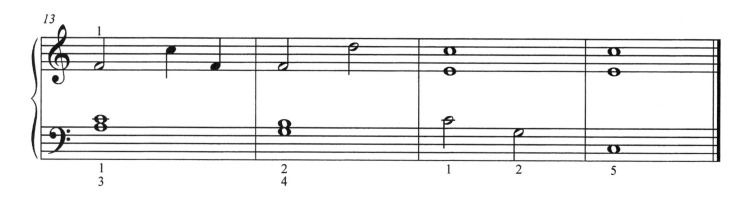

Ramble

Fishel Pustilnik

Brightly, with a beat

Frozen Full Moon on a Sunday Afternoon

Joyce Pinckney

Jazz Waltz style (accent the second beat)

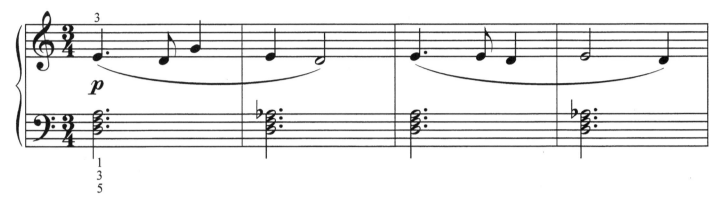

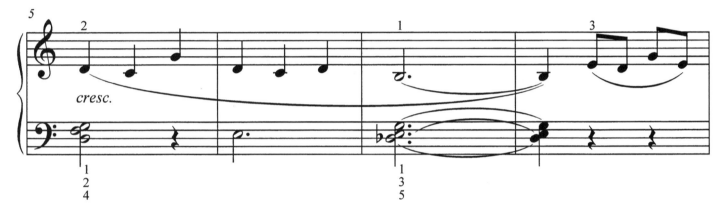

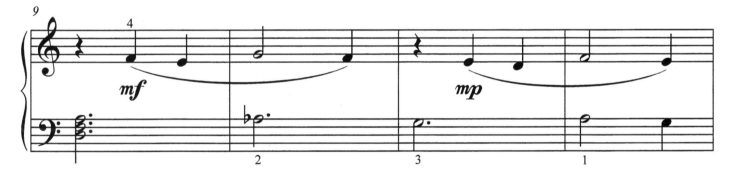

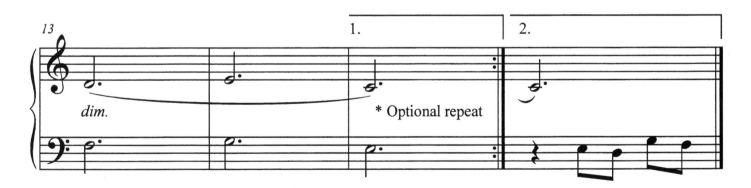

*Optional repeat: Change the left hand by silently depressing a five-note cluster from C to G.
Hold the cluster for the entire piece to create a mystical and mysterious sound.

Got the Blues

Andrew Harbridge

Not too fast (swing the 8ths)

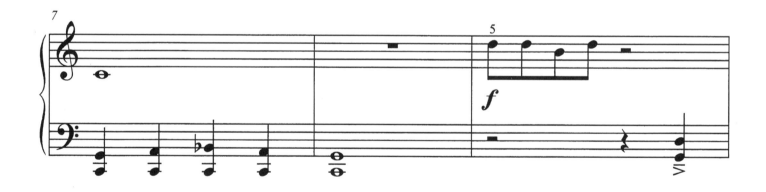

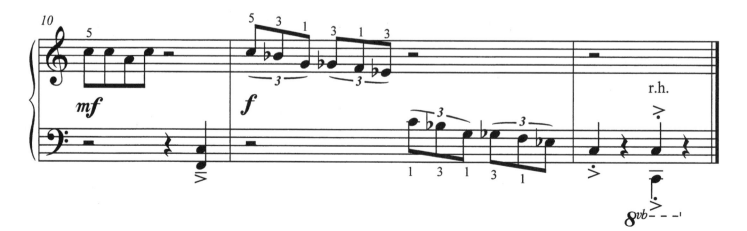

Rainy Day Rag

Debra Wanless

Rag Style, not too fast

l.h. slightly detached

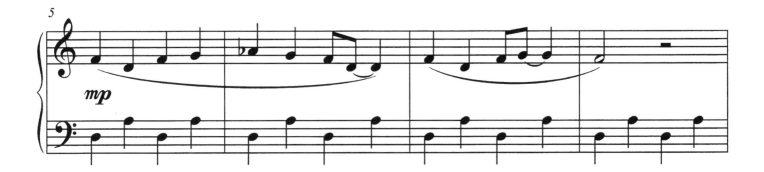

On My Way

Tyler Seidenberg

With a lilt (swing the 8ths)

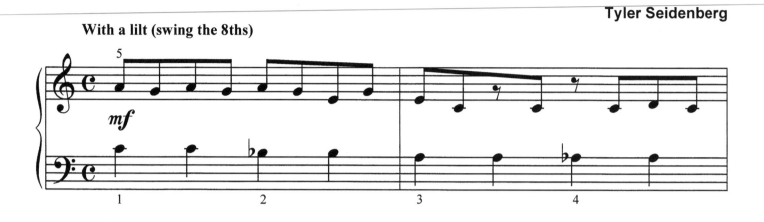

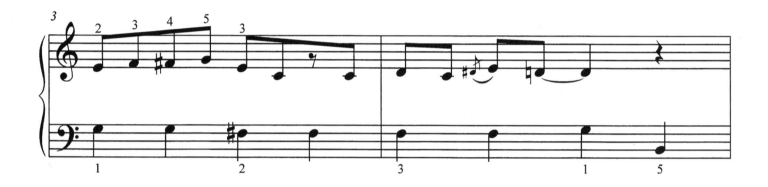

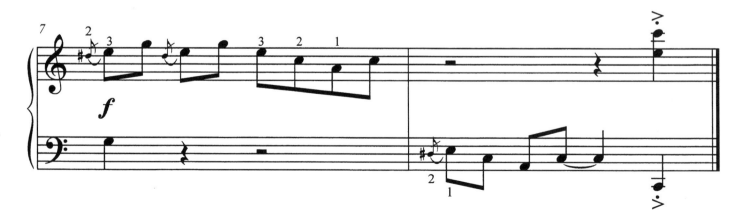

Kind Wishes

Fishel Pustilnik

Bass Boogie

Robert Benedict

Not Too Fast (swing the 8ths)

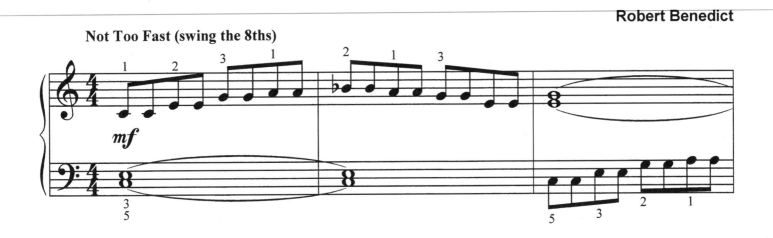

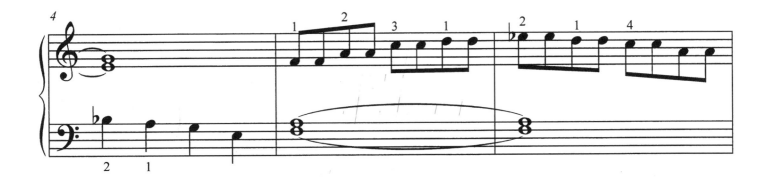

Blues In My Soul

Fishel Pustilnik

Easy Swing (swing the 8ths)

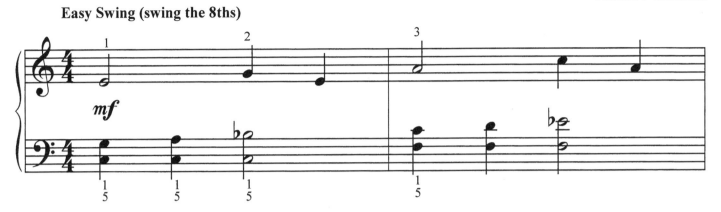

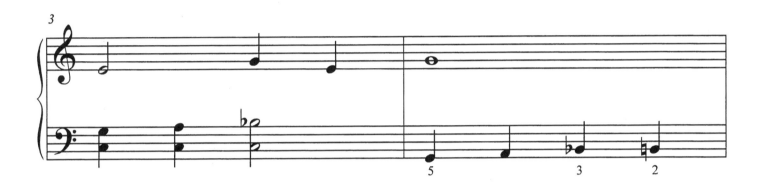

Cowboy's Song

Andrew Harbridge

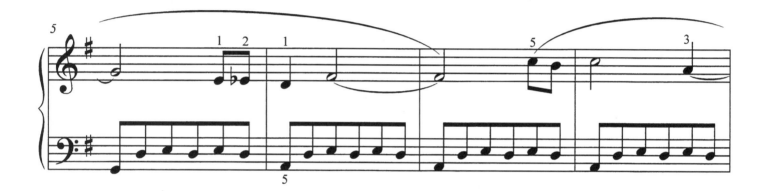

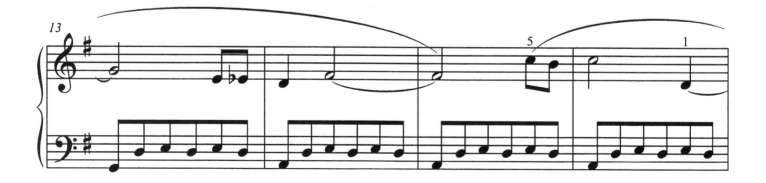

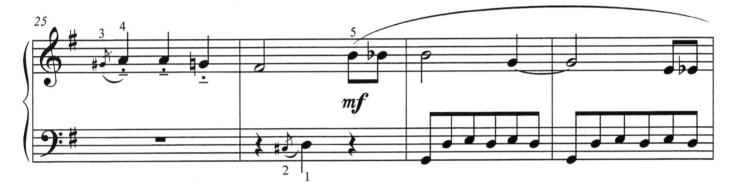

Cowboy's Song 2 / 2

Icicle Rag

Joyce Pinckney

Not too fast

(l.h. slightly detached)

Saga

Fishel Pustilnik

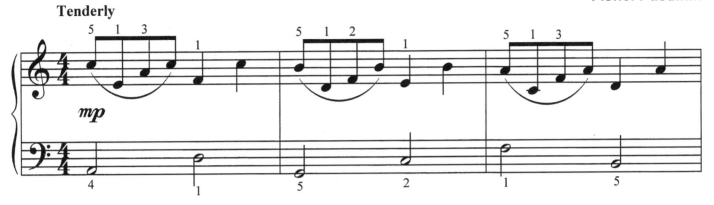

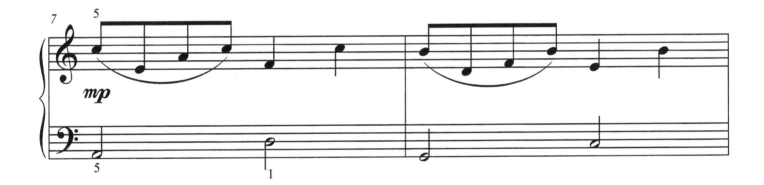

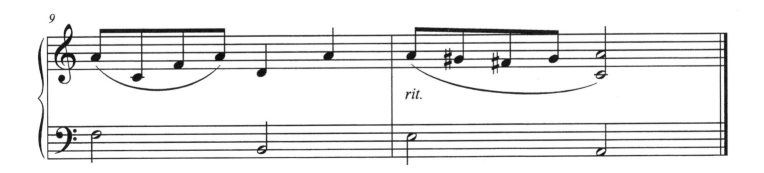

Otonabee River Song

Andrew Harbridge

Gently Flowing

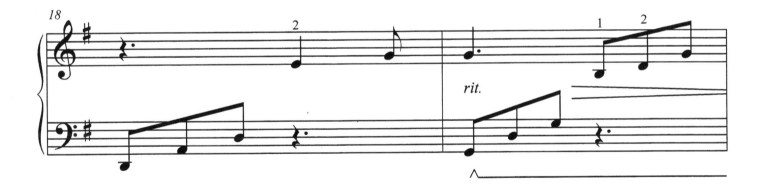

Otonabee River Song 2 / 2

Aeolian Jazz Waltz

Andrew Harbridge

Not too fast

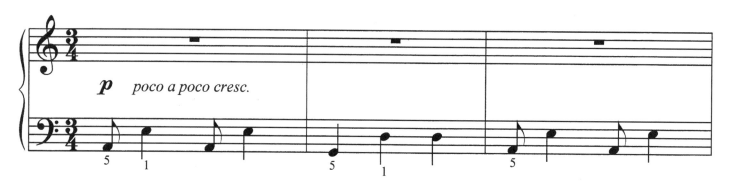

Aeolian Jazz Waltz 2 / 2

Sunflowers and Sage Brush

Joyce Pinckney

Warmly (Straight 8ths)

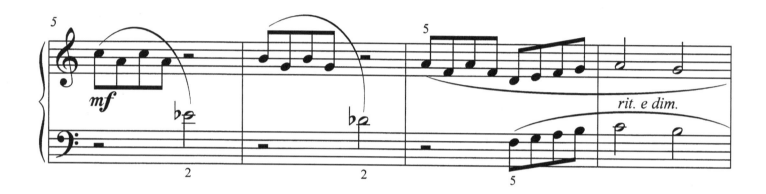

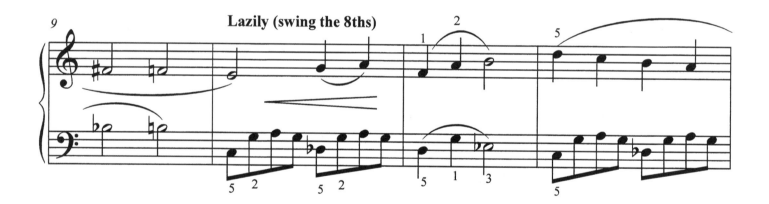

Lazily (swing the 8ths)

Dinosaur Disco

Janet Gieck

Moderately, with a steady beat

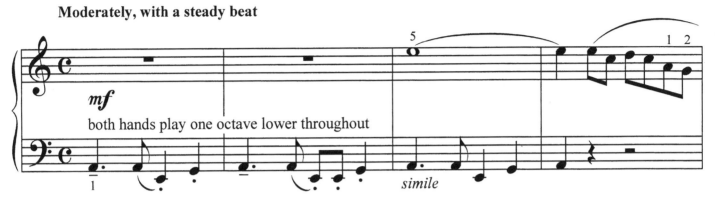

both hands play one octave lower throughout

Brave Wolfe

Canadian Folk Song
adapted from Fowke/Johnston

Mournfully

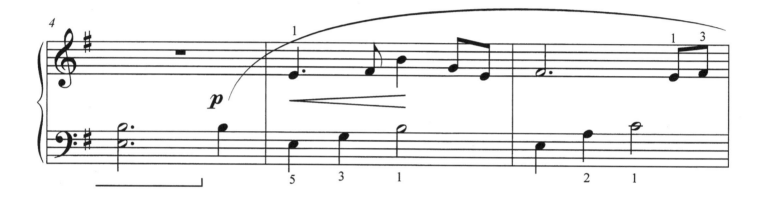

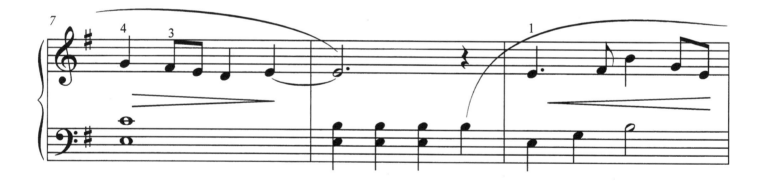

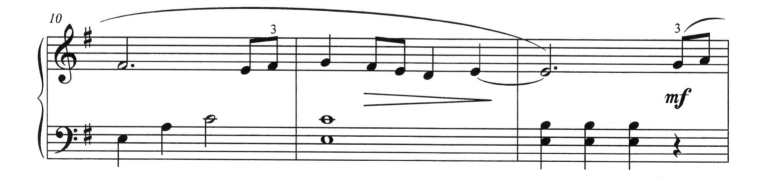

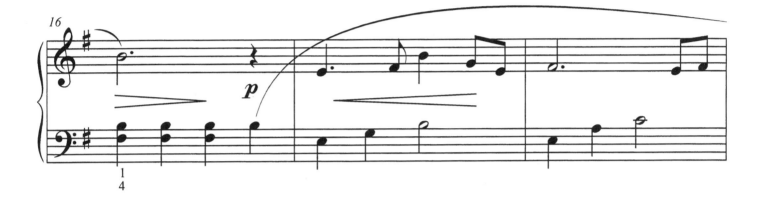

Brave Wolfe 2 / 2

Hush Now

for Marga

Joyce Pinckney

Gently (swing the 8ths)

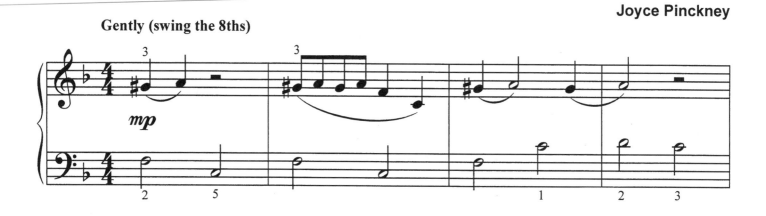

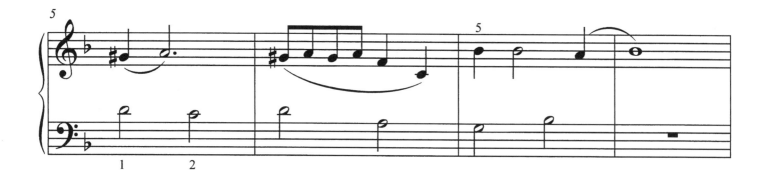

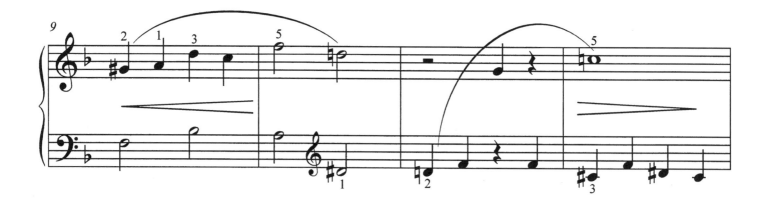

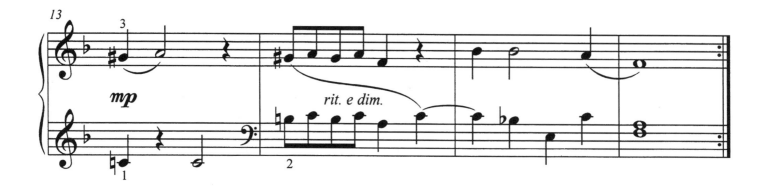

Ace of Spades

It's Your Deal

Tyler Seidenberg

Cool and Jazzy (swing the 8ths)

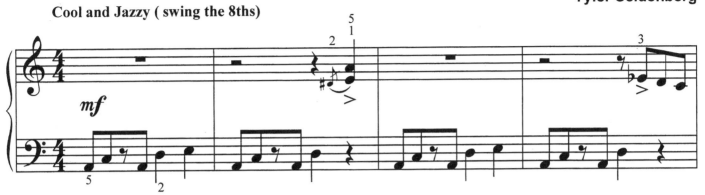

Olé

Rémi Bouchard

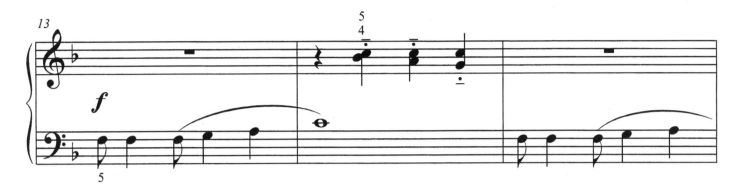

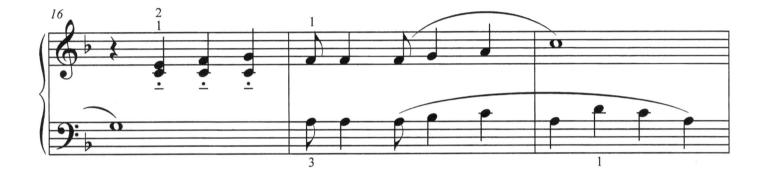

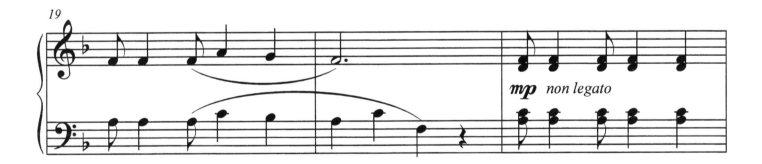

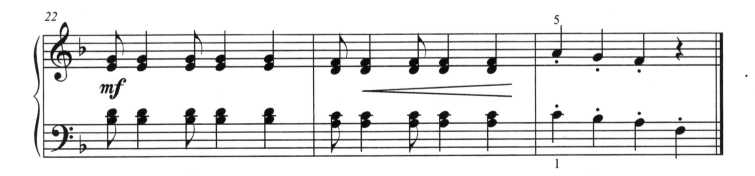

Ole 2 / 2

Cheetah Cha Cha

John Sandy

Hotly

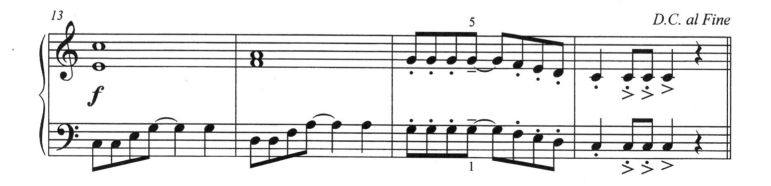

Citadel Hill

Canadian Folk Song
adapted from Fowke/Johnston

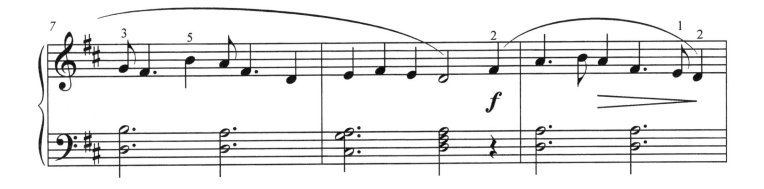

Snow Angel

Janet Gieck

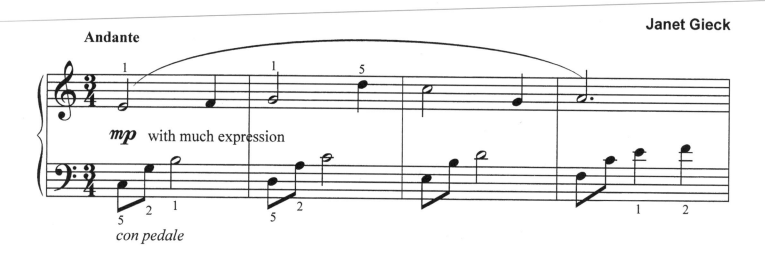

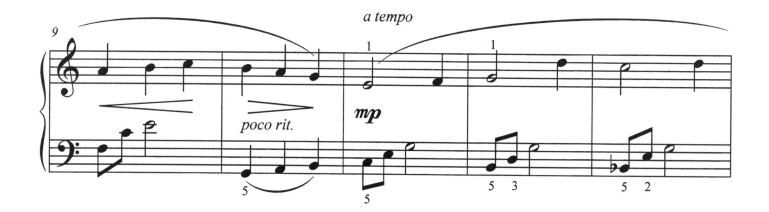

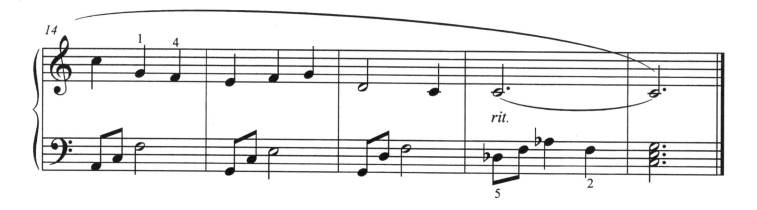

Glossary of Jazz Idioms

Ballad – is a slow jazz work characterized by a lyrical melody.

Blues – is a jazz style generally for solo voice. It was often sad and slow, usually utilizing the blues scale or notes and a twelve bar harmonic structure.

Blues Scale – is a predominantly major scale with a flattened third, fifth and seventh notes.

Boogie-Woogie – is a jazz style for the piano with a repeated left hand pattern. Boogie-woogie developed in dance halls during the 1920's and often uses the *twelve bar blues* harmonic structure.

Diatonic Seventh Chords - consist of four notes, a triad with the seventh added above the root. Diatonic seventh chords use only the notes of the scale.

Dixieland – is a type of jazz from around 1912 and is also known as New Orleans or Classic style jazz. It has elements of *ragtime* and *blues*, as well as a distinctive style of *improvisation.*

Improvisation - is a spontaneous production of musical ideas by the performer.

Modes - musical scales developed from early church music, often used and modified by classical and jazz composers. Folk music is often written in modal keys.

Ostinato - is a repeated harmonic, rhythmic or melodic pattern.

Pentatonic Scale - is a scale of five notes, often representing the intervals of the five black keys on the piano. Pentatonic scales are frequently heard in folk music and non-western music.

Ragtime – is one of the earliest forms of jazz, characterized by *syncopated* melodies, *stride bass* and traditional harmonies.

Rock - is a popular style of dance music that developed during the 1950's and is usually based on even eighth note subdivisions. Rock is the simplest derivation of Latin rhythms.

Shuffle Bass – a jazz accompaniment which moves or shuffles back and forth between the same notes.

Stride Bass – is an accompaniment pattern usually found in *ragtime*. It describes the striding motion of the player's left hand.

Swing Rhythm – is a rhythmic technique which grew out the big band era and dance music of the 1930's and 1940's. Rhythm is swung when the beat note is stretched to create a 'long-short' combination. Example:

Syncopation – is the alteration of the natural accent by emphasizing and normally weak beat.

Twelve-Bar Blues - in its simplest form, is a harmonic pattern organized into three four bar phrases. The harmonic pattern is as follows: I - I - I - I   IV - IV - I - I   V - IV - I - I
Colour tones, altered and seventh chords are often included within the pattern.

Glossary

SIGN	TERM	DEFINITION
(accent sign)	accent	Emphasize the marked note
	andante	Rather slow, a walking pace
	a tempo	Return to the original speed or tempo
	con	With
(crescendo sign)	crescendo/cresc.	Gradually become louder
D.C.	Da capo	Repeat from the beginning
(diminuendo sign)	diminuendo/dim.	Gradually become softer
	e	And
(1st 2nd ending sign)	1st and 2nd ending	Play the first ending and repeat. Then skip the first ending and play the second ending instead
(fermata sign)	fermata	Pause on the note or rest
	fine	The end
f	forte	Loud
(glissando sign)	glissando	Drag the finger across the keys
(grace note sign)	grace note	Play the small note as quickly as possible, immediately
l.h.	left hand	Play with the left hand
r.h.	right hand	Play with the right hand
	legato	Smoothly
	leggiero	Lightly
mf	mezzo forte	Medium loud
mp	mezzo piano	Medium soft
	non	Not
8va----- 8vb-----	ottava	Play one octave higher than written Play one octave lower than written
‖: :‖	repeat signs	Repeat the section within the repeat sign
(pedale sign)	pedale	Depress the damper or right hand pedal
pp	pianissimo	Very soft
p	piano	soft
	poco a poco	Little by little
rit.	ritard. / ritardando	Gradually becoming slower
	senza	Without
	simile	The same
(staccato sign)	staccato	Play the notes short and detached
	tenuto	Sustained
(triplet sign)	triplet	Three notes played in the value of two
	Vivo	Fast, lively